love is nothing but a cycle of disappointment

Carter Elise Key

BookLeaf Publishing

love is nothing but a cycle of disappointment

Presentation by *BookLeaf Publishing*

Web: www.bookleafpub.com

E-mail: info@bookleafpub.com

ISBN: 9789357446815

First edition 2022

DEDICATION

To everyone who doesn't know if they'll be able to make it through the night

because a lover has hurt them

because their pets are with their parents

because they don't know how to reach out for help

may you escape for a while,

and live vicariously through my words,

because I promise.

You will make it through the night.

the words you ~~won't~~ don't say are almost as loud as the words you do

things i wish you would've said but didn't:
- "i trust you"
- "i'd love a hug from you"
- "yes"
- "you're enough"
- "i'm proud of you"
- "thank you"
- "i'd miss you"
- "your hard work is paying off"
- "i can't wait to see what you become"
- "please"
- "carter!"
- "carter—"
- "carter?"
- "carter."
- "you amuse me"
- "i like the way you ____"
- "what do you want to do?"
- "could i talk to you about this?"
- "tell me more"
- "i really like this!"
- "i enjoy your writing"
- "this made me think of you"
- "text me when you get to your apartment"
- "let me know when you're free"
- "how are you doing, really?"

only princesses in faerietales get happy endings, not college students in the real world

I've finally found a reason to write again.
My emotions are finally
gut-wrenching
sobbing
feeling numb and
everything at once
again.
I was a fool to think that
you
would be the one to stick around
that you
were going to be
the relationship to end all relationships
the one I could call my forever
the person I could trust
and treasure
and plan with
and love
for the rest of my life.
Because you,
yes, you, the one I planned the next
lifetime and a half with
because I thought this was it
and we were being honest with each other

about what we wanted out of this
goddamn relationship,
but you wanted something different
than what you've been
telling me
for the past
lifetime,
no,
year and a half that felt like a lifetime
because I thought it was going to be
the beginning of one
I thought…
I thought I was done with heartbreak
and I thought I could venture into
the unknown waters of finally feeling
loved.
But we all know that
I'm never going to actually get
a happy ending.
You fooled me
into believing that I was finally
getting that.
I thought my tragic life
was finally changing course
to blossom into
one of the best love stories ever written
where we loved each other through
a fucking worldwide pandemic
and

me
finally becoming comfortable with who I am
and ending the eternal unknowing of going
through
an identity crisis that lasted seven years
and you loved me.
Even when I felt unlovable.
Because I finally started to process my trauma
surrounding relationships
in therapy
to help me become a more whole person
in order to love you the way
I thought
you deserved to be loved.
But all of a sudden
summer is over
and you've come to some sort of
"reality check"
that what you want
isn't
me
anymore.
What you want is nothing I can provide for you
and when I proposed coming with you,
because I thought you were the goddamn
endgame,
you said "no.
"i mean i'll be leaving
right after i graduate.

"And you'll still be
"here…
"For another three years."
Even though none of that is
guaranteed
and
that was never
part of any plan
we had ever talked about.
"But I still want to be friends."
…
"I just want to be really good
"friends
"with you
"for my senior year."
…
Ouch.
That was a lot of damage.
I'll need some time but
I'll respect your wishes,
and set up boundaries
to help me
backtrack
to the time before I loved you.
Because unloving you
is going to be
one of the most difficult things
I've ever done
in my entire

short
lifetime here
on this godforsaken earth.

forgive me father for i have sinned in idolizing my lover

it was never if--
it was always when
when we get married,
when we have kids,
when we move in together and
get a medium-sized dog and
a fluffy maine coon half-breed because
we adopt don't shop in this household.
i had never had a doubt
in my mind
that we would be there for each other,
that you are my person.
...were my person now, I guess.
because now I'm sitting,
eating french fries on the edge of holy land,
listening to loud-engined cars pass by and
conversations had by strangers because
my mind won't stop drowning
in silence.
in the complete and utter lack of
you.

i could make a home in your eyes but i don't want to move out of where i am now

oops!

...fuck.

I did it again
because I don't know how to just
be friends
with people
again
and I don't know how to handle
or even process
really being hurt--
because believe me,
it still fucking hurts.

But the way that you make me smile
and the way that you warm parts of me
that I didn't even know had gone cold,
and the way that your eyes light up
even when you're trying to hide a smile
after I say something dumb or amusing or
something you find funny.
the way that I
literally
get lost in your eyes
because they're so dark and large
that they're like unexplored caves

waiting for someone to settle in
and call them "home".
The way that when I call you
"my love"
your face softens just a bit
and your posture relaxes
and it's almost like you want to start calling me
"home"
too.

Maybe it's because I have a history
of only ever being "almosts" or "maybes"
with Scorpio men
but maybe,
goddammit maybe,
I don't want this one to be that
anymore
and I want to break my streak
of nights I cry myself to sleep
or at least
stop scrolling through tiktok until I find a sound
monotonous enough that I stop scrolling and let
it play out until I eventually just pass out.

I want to have
a bed partner
again.
I want to have someone
who will stay with me when it's a bad day

and celebrate with me when it's a good day.
I want someone to run their
gentle fingers
through my tangled hair;
I want a reason to shower again.

Holding
eye contact
with you
is so difficult because whenever
I enter those caves it becomes
a game of who will break
away first and I never want it to be
me. I hope you're out sailing
on the oceans or surfing on clouds
in the skies that are my eyes
but gods above
it's like we were night and day,
made to love each other...

but I don't think this timeline is for us.

As much as I want it to be,
I just don't know what would come of it.

thunder rolling ; blood rushing ; bells tolling ; thighs brushing

All that I can hear tonight
is the thunder rolling across the
sky like the blood rushing in
my ears and it's taking every ounce of my
physical strength to force myself
to focus and not float back to
the night when that
happened or the time that

you told me I looked good even though
I wasn't yours to tell that to or even
the time when our legs kept
brushing under the current of the waves
and the ocean felt so, so nice.
and I had been burnt a few days before.
you kept offering to put aloe on
the scaly skin that was healing...
and you made sure to try and take care of me,
even though I put up the front that it wasn't me
who needed taking care of.
I was fine, handling it by myself and with the
help
of someone I thought I would be loving

forever oh no it's happening again we're

floating back to that place through
time and space and i can't seem to get my
head wrapped around where I am now and how
the thunder sounds and never
really knowing which way is
up or down or right or left or understanding
when we're flirting and when we're
not oh my god oh my god oh my

god
oh my god
we were flirting
we were flirting back and forth,
I'm sure of it.

I could conquer any part of myself
as long as I knew that you were there,
supporting me,
whether it be from a distance
or right there by my side.

we were flirting.

oh my god,
I want you.

i chronically think that i'm a bother and you declined my request to hang out a bit too abruptly

oh shit,
did I do something wrong?

last night,
when we were together,
i had never felt more
intimate
with a single person
having not even lost
any of my clothing.

I felt
so light,
and so free,
but also chained down by the reality of my
situation
all at once.

i think i finally understood
what Jack felt at the end of
the titanic movie.

i even read my poetry to you,
nothing recent

because you can't know what those
are
yet.

i mentioned that i write and
this got brought up and
you asked for a preview of what was to come,
so i let you scroll through the archives
of my own damned heart
and choose what you wanted me to read aloud
with the caveat that
you don't scroll to the top of the blog.
luckily for me,
and luckily for you, i guess,
because i have no idea how you'd react to these
poems
(hell, i don't even know how i'm reacting to
these poems)
you didn't!
you respected my wish,

at least, i think you did,
because there wasn't any sort of
heavily awkward silence
that happens when you know that
when
ah damn, it's even difficult to type it out.
none of those
pregnant silences

of contemplation
when you know the person sitting in the driver's
seat

likes? has a crush on?
could picture themselves being happy with?
both actively and passively wants a relationship
with?
loves?

you. and
and it isn't like you could just
up and leave, we were sitting in the parking lot
of the zoo
until almost four in the morning,
that's not walking distance from your house.
but i feel like i did something.

i feel like i

dammit
my vision is blurring and i can't see the
keyboard.

something's wrong,
and i need to fix it.

fuck.

my life flashed before my eyes & i wasn't even actually dying, what a bummer

"Babes huh?"
I saw your name pop up on my screen
but that was definitely not the text i was
expecting
panic
oh my god so much panic
heat plagued my face,
i'm pretty sure even my ears turned red,
my vision blurred out for a second
panic mode activated
i threw my phone at the person sitting next to me
and cried "help"

"...yes?
"do you not want me to call you that?"
even more panic

oh my god

i can't believe i actually responded
i should have left you on read
i shouldn't have gotten so excited
flustered
been so caught off guard

i guess since i call all my friends "babes"
it wouldn't be that big of a deal
but you didn't look over it
and oh my god you didn't look over it

pacing

pacing

pacing

talking with my hands
need to get this nervous energy
o u t
somehow

pacing

my friend made me tea
and i'm so incredibly thankful,
the tea was so good and it was
just how i like it.

"Carter,
"don't look at the phone."
i can't help it

dammit

i keep looking over at the phone

trying to figure out what
the hell
kind of response you'd have because
all three of us read that message
in a teasing tone
because damn,

it's difficult to convey tone over text.

i keep thinking i hear
buzzes
and i don't have my watch on
so i can't even double check
to make sure i'm not hallucinating
because i just want a goddamn answer already
holy shit
holy fuck
i moved the stuffie covering the screen and

oh my god
your name
it's there
quick unlock the phone
what does it say
what doesn't it say

"Preferably not"

oh shit

oh fuck
i messed up
oh shit
more panic
my heart and soul are sinking
it's lay on the floor time
how the
fuck
do i respond to that?
huh?
what do you want me to say?
i fucking—

god this is so childish

"oh my bad
"i call all of my good friends babes"
send.

fuck
oh my god oh my
shit shit shit

lay on the floor,
get wrapped in a weighted blanket
and handed an emotional support stuffie
and sit.

try not to cry

try not to laugh
try not to anything because
i don't know how the hell to react to that
my heart is still beating
a million miles a minute,
my ears are still red,
my throat is still tight.

it's all that i can think of
that stupid text

god, i was so dumb to text you in the first place.
i knew you'd be busy
i knew you'd be drinking

maybe that's part of why i texted you in the first
place,
because one time
you told me you were a sad drunk
and i wanted to make sure
that you were
just
fucking
okay.

well, now don't be surprised if i just don't
initiate any contact until this stupid book is
published

or until i’ve been resurrected from my
embarrassment
because oh my god

all of your texts tonight—
three, to be precise—
were just two words at a time
and it still felt like every single letter
was just volley after volley of

hurt.
excitement.
hope.
anxiety.
and oh my god

i never want to ride that roller coaster again.

jrr tolkein once said "not all those who wander are lost" and i like to believe that applies to my dreams

I wake up from a dream
where you're cradling my face
in calloused hands with
slender fingers
tracing their way up my
jawline and beginning to tangle
into my dirty, unkept hair.
I shiver,
the sensation sending xylophone taps
up each every one of my vertebrae.
your fingers lock in
at the base of my hairline.
my eyes widen,
remaining locked with yours.
the pools of almost-blackness
sweep me away into a
peaceful unknown.
i wish that i could have stayed in this moment
forever
frozen in time
floating here
no other feelings besides
your slender fingers in my hair,
my hand pressed lightly against

your hardened chest
feeling your heartbeat through
a thin layer of cotton,
and the sensation of being

lost

and

found

all at once.

i don't know how to process any of the feelings i'm having and it scares me to death

do i actually like you, or do you just have
fluffy dark hair
and
really pretty eyes?

do i actually like you, or are you just
only vaguely emotionally available,
and continue to hang out with me
whenever i pester you into doing so…
…because i like you.

wait, what?

do i actually like you, or do you just have
awesome facial hair
that i really want to braid?

do i actually like you or do you just look
really good
in a swimsuit?

do i actually like you, or do i just
post things for you to watch to my story
even though i know you never watch my story

so it's just me
ranting
about how you have such a positive impact
on my life…
and then you'll never know it,
because you never watch my stories?

do i actually like you, or did i just
like the way you reacted
when i read my poetry to you?

do i actually like you, or do you just
respect my boundaries
and have set up boundaries that i
respect
in turn?

do i actually like you or do i just
really
want a hug from you?

do i actually like you or do i just think
you'd be
really
really good
at kissing?

do i actually like you or do you just
know how to play the video games that i want

to get good at?
and can teach me?
(that's actually a new one
so congrats on unlocking it
i guess)

do i actually like you, or do you just
have a really pretty voice?

do i actually like you....
yeah that's it that's all for this one it's just
"do i like you?"

do i like you, or can you just
match my sarcasm
and make it clear when you're being sarcastic
so that I don't feel
self-conscious?

do i actually like you, or do i just
really
want you to model for me?

do i actually like you, or do we just
order the same thing at mcdonald's every time
because
out of all the people i know,
i've never met someone that also gets the
quarter pounder with cheese meal

with no modifications and
a sprite. you're the only one.

do i like you, or am i just
not over my ex yet?
because i had a crush on you
when we first met,
and then we never started talking,
and now that's back!
because you're more attractive,
and i am heartbroken.

do i actually like you, or did we just
have DnD characters that were friends?
and i kind of wanted to make it a
romantic relationship
because i thought that it would be funny
because a little
rabbit man
and a human
with the little rabbit man pining after the human
would have actually been
kind of funny,
but then I didn't because
my ex was running the campaign,
and I didn't know what he would think of that.

do I actually like you, or do i just feel the
consistent need

to take care of you?
because you told me that you were a sad drunk
once
at Sebastian's birthday party,
and now every time that you mention
that you're drinking,
oh boy do I feel the need to text you and be like:

"hey are you okay you're doing okay you're not sad right you're chilin you're good awesome do you need anything do you need food hangover medicine cure i can i can also provide hugs and moderate emotional availability if you need to talk about anything because i…

"i value your life."

do i actually like you, or do i think that
you could pick me up
and throw me?

do i actually like you, or do i just think that
you would be a really interesting main character
in an anime?

do i actually like you, or do you just have
the healthy relationship with all of your family
that i wish that i
could have?

do i actually like you, or is it just
really easy
to write poetry about you?

do i actually like you, or is
your hair just
soft?
and salt and pepper textured?

do i actually like you, or do i kind of
get a little bit of a thrill
from doing shit like this,
knowing that you are going to be reading this
book
and knowing that you won't react to it
until it hits the shelves,
whenever that is,
but it's okay! it's okay,
it helps me emotionally to write down my
feelings.

do i actually like you, or have i just
trained myself to think
that everyone likes me
first
because it's safer that way?
and there was a period in high school
where it was proven

because i had like
twenty people
confess feelings for me over the span of
two weeks,
and i don't know what kind of crack those
people were on
but now my brain is like

"wow! you're out of a relationship. every single
person that you interact with has a crush on you
probably, and that's really rough buddy"

so do i just think that
you like me,
and that i could be happy in a relationship with
you
or do i actually like you?

do i actually like you, or can you just
cook?

do i actually like you, or could i just
start picturing a domestic life
with you,
and that would be pretty cool?
(i do think that if we lived together,
it would be a pretty
symbiotic
relationship.)

do i actually like you, or do i think that
my cat
would like you
if you ever met her?

do i actually like you, or do you just
smell nice?

do i actually like you, or do i just
have gender envy for you?
because you are very pretty.

do i actually like you, or do i just
think it's pretty awesome
when you laugh?

do i actually like you, or do we just
have the same sense of humour?

and alright guys,
here's the big one:

do i actually like you,
or am i just afraid that you're going to leave me
once you graduate–
like all of my other friends are–
and the only way that I know how to make you
stay…

is to get into a relationship with you?

i like having control but i hate having power

by showing me
little previews
of how you see the world
you've given me
insight
on how to
hurt you.
how to most effectively
push
          you
                    away,
should i ever feel the need.
should there be any reason
why i feel like i'm being a
toxic
thorn in your side,
i know how to make you remove me.
even if you may not
want to.
i'm so fucking afraid
of getting close to people—

and you,
oh god
          you

terrify
me—

i have to keep myself from picking up these
destructive habits,
forcing myself to be the opposite
of everything you hold dear.
it's ugly,
how quickly these shifts can occur.
would you recognize
me
once i shroud myself in
fear
hatred
toxicity
and every word is coated with
slick
venom?
i could make you hate me.
i could
definitely
make you
hate me.

and i think that power terrifies me more than i'd
like to admit.

this mcdonalds is something i'm always going to connect to you now

i was driving them to the mcdonalds we've taken
to frequenting on nights when i need you,
and you seem happy to oblige.
the windows were down,
they were blasting music,
i was probably going a bit over the speed limit—
but it's new jersey,
who actually drives the speed limit here?—
and the frigid wind kept a cold grip
on my neck, the feeling of icicles clasping
right where your face, fingers, palm could fit
like a perfectly made key to unlock
a treasure trove of uncertainty and
rigid recollections
because i don't want to get hurt again

but for you…

whatever happens when
this freefall pauses,
it'll be worth it.

it'll all be worth it.

playlists can lend themselves to some pretty intense memories, if you're creative enough

there are two playlists that seem to be
on repeat
for me
these past few days.

"a mixtape for a nonexistent lover"

and

"if my life were a movie this would be the
soundtrack"

granted,
there are some songs that overlap,
because what's a good
indie
coming-of-age
movie
without some heartbreak?
some romance?
some quirky
gay
songs
about how awesome it would be

if i could actually love
every
single
person
who's caused me to put a song on that
playlist?

i can name the people who have inspired the
conscious structure
of curated emotions that flow into

"a mixtape for a nonexistent lover"

and i've been adding to that playlist
since i began it
march 2nd, 2018

that playlist is coming up on being
four years old.

i started it
the spring of
my junior year of high school.

i could probably tell you
the exact person,
moment,
thought,
that made me add

each and every
song
to that stupid playlist.

and hell,
the songs he associated me with
when i asked him to send me something
something that reminded him of me,
something that i could hold onto,
while i was in the
city of love
feeling everything but.

the very first song
that started this playlist
was for my very best friend.

he had just told me that
he had a crush on me,
when we first met,
and that he thinks he's bi.

his girlfriend didn't react awesome
to either of those statements,
and i told him that it was okay.

he was okay.

he was doing awesome.

I Know How It Ends by Samsa,
which,
unfortunately,
isn't available on spotify anymore.

but i'm never removing it.

the song that
a summer love
used to sing to me,
that even though
we aren't on great terms,
it's still my favourite
Elton John
song.

he used to tell me that
one day,
when he's rich and famous,
we can travel the world...
or just coexist in the same space.

he would be happy with
whatever.

Your Song by Elton John.

every time I hear it,

i'm transported back
to summer car rides
and
sunflower fields,
and then later--
singing that same song
to Jake
sitting on the floor of the kitchen
while he made
steak and mashed potatoes
for dinner
and i'm certainly no cook,
but he wanted the company,
and he wanted music.

so i gave it to him.

i certainly don't pride myself
on my voice,
but it was enough.

it was enough for him.

i don't think i'll ever
dance around in refrigerator light
to classic rock
at three in the morning
while wearing the oversized clothing
of whatever lover i may have,

but damn.
a bitch can dream.

i could be the Eugene to your Rapunzel if only you'd let me

i think the most
disheartening
thing about the way that the audience knows that
the prince really does love the princess
is by looking at the way he watches her
when she's preoccupied by something
beautiful.

what the hell sort of
dramatic irony
is that.

she never knows.

the people on the receiving ends of these
longing stares that are full of so much
hope and love
never even know when they're happening.

i know how
beautiful
it is to watch someone experience what they're
passionate about
or to watch someone's eyes
light up

in recognition and then wait as they tell
their own story.

my friends are so incredibly
awe-inspiring
(i like to think i have good taste)
but holy shit oh my god i don't think
i don't think i've ever been
someone
who inspires that level of pure intrigue
or commands attention like that—
i don't think i'm passionate
enough.

and of course,
you could tell me that i am.
i'd probably think
you're just saying that
because now you have access
to this stupid fucking blog
and you read my poetry
on a daily basis—
hell, you have this page open
on safari right now—
but you can.
and if you do,
maybe i won't feel so
insignificant,
or maybe i won't

believe you
and then i'll try to slowly
wedge my way out of
your life because i
realise that
i've become
a burden.

the language of love is one that perpetually perplexes me

i wonder which love language covers

- sending you memes on instagram that i think you'll find funny
- consistently wondering how your mood is today (i always hope you're doing well)
- seeking approval through the tiniest of actions, and especially reading into them
- wanting to understand the intricacies of your mind, but also wanting to memorize the feeling of your arms wrapped around me
- even though we've never hugged before
- trying my best to make sure you know that i love you without saying the words, because you told me that whenever i'm affectionate towards you it makes you uncomfortable
- just wanting to exist
- together.

as someone who prides themself on their
knowledge of languages,
the intricacies of communication,
the base of human connection...
please tell me what
box
this fits into.

distance can't dictate the fact that i still fucking love you

we facetimed tonight.
it was the first time
since i had you call me
to get out of jake's house
almost a month ago.

you were drunk,
and taking an exam
due at 10 am later today.

you also took the quiz
to find out what your
hogwarts house is.
the quiz gave you gryffindor,
but i'm calling bullshit.
when you were taking it
the quiz asked what kind of owl
you'd take with you.
"that one looks like a friend,
"i'll take that one"

that's some hufflepuff shit
if i've ever heard it.

then, once the result popped up

"ron wesley" had us cracking up
for ten minutes straight.

i couldn't breathe.

we talked about how horny the guys
on yikyak at your campus are.
we talked about your professor.
we talked about how your school
won a huge game last night
and apparently someone streaked
through the math building
butt ass naked
today.

you kept making references
that i didn't understand
and then you'd send the source material
and i'd start fucking cackling
and then you'd start smiling.

god,
i missed that smile.

i missed the way our eyes mirror each other,
neighbouring areas of the same vast ocean,
both startling and intriguing
sharing thoughts on a wavelength
uninterrupted

since i met you my sophomore year.

i hate
so much
that i have to watch you
suffer
from afar
and that i can’t
be there
to give you the hugs
and forehead kisses
that you deserve

(even if i’d have to stand on
an elevated surface for the
forehead
kisses).

you need to weed your garden regularly in order to keep up the pretty picture

the long answer--
'good'
is relative.

'good'
can be leaving a situation that no longer helps
you grow.
can be escaping from ugly parts of yourself.
can be understanding that this place isn't yours
to occupy
anymore.

'good'
should not be mourning mornings where you're
not with me.
should not be making my clothes ill-fitting
because
    i feel like i don't deserve my meals.
    i'm not that hungry anymore.
    the only reason i ate was because
    you cooked.
i don't know what else to do.

'good'
is benevolent.

is amicable.
is a clean break,
with closure.

'bye', on the other hand, is not so relative.
'bye' is watching the way your shoulders bounce
with every step that you take
a w a y
from me.
'bye' is a hug for the last time,
crying into your shoulder for the last time,
feeling suffocated and encased in your arms for
the last time,
even though that sensation was once one of
safety and comfort.

maybe that's why
i don't really like hugs,
unless they're from exactly
one
person.
and i don't know if i'm quite there yet.

huh.

anyways,
the short answer--

the only 'good' part of 'goodbye' is that you vacated my life to make room for something new, something lovely, something you may have seen coming and neglected to address.

you left.
and i'm finally starting to be okay with that.

shall i compare thee to a summer night?

it's almost 6:30 in the morning.
the sun rises in
about twenty minutes.

you told me that
you didn't want to stay out much longer
because you couldn't force yourself to stay up
to watch the sunrise.

now i can see in my apartment
without even turning on any artificial light,
and part of me hopes that you're asleep
and you passed out as soon as i
dropped you off
and you actually left my car
after sitting in a comfortable silence,
and speaking only when necessary.

i've written about how your eyes remind me
of the night sky,
pools of deep brown
(almost black)
that are as vast and expansive as
the universe,
but i think for the first time
today,

i realized that you're so full of light
that your eyes must need to dim some of it,
otherwise your presence would be
blinding
as opposed to the
comfort
that it is.

even though we're not watching
this sunrise together,
it's comforting to know that
we're under the same sky.

you almost fell asleep
in the passenger's seat of
my car,
but a part of me wonders
if you, too, were unable
to force yourself to sleep
before seeing the sun break over the horizon to
the east.

i hope you get a great sleep tonight
and that maybe
you aren't sick of me yet,
and i'll get to be with you again
tomorrow.

to hell with where i am now ; home is a person and that person is you

"do you want to do
one more
reading,
or do you want to
head back
for the night?"

big stretch.

yawn.

"you seem pretty
tired."

"no,
you."

you folded your arms across your chest,
sparing a playful glance to look my way.
i don't remember what my face must have
looked like,
but it made you smile,
and we broke out into laughter.

"no, seriously.
do you want to head back?"

"we can do
one
more
reading,
and then let's head home."

my heart
fractured
in that moment.

i hope you couldn't see it on my face but
you just said
"let's head home."

my love.
the closest concept that i have to
"home"
now exists in
throwing french fries at you
whenever you do something to mildly
inconvenience or irritate me,
and watching you get excited
because you get more food out of this trip now.
"home" exists in the space between

"i'm here!"
and
"got back safe"

texts.

i’m so transient that i don’t have a place to call
“home,”
only pockets of time and space
i can steal,
we can share,
that bring me the sense of safety
i’ve always believed
“home”
to be

i may not have an awesome understanding of how to deal with my emotions, but i at least got this down pat

sometimes i wonder if you hate being talked over because you're used to being the loudest person in the room. sometimes i wonder if you get tired from constantly trying to one-up everyone around you. sometimes i wonder if you even realise that you're doing it. sometimes i wonder if you're able to pick up on the fact that you're not funny or witty or likeable by consistently correcting others on their pieces of knowledge or making pop culture references that one person doesn't get and then you get frustrated with the fact that they don't understand it and tear down their experiences.

sometimes i wonder…
…but wondering is useless.

i just want something that was
not... that
because tonight was really
not the night for that
since i missed your text
and then i almost fucking
died

and i don't know why
you don't see me as a nuisance
but i know how to use it to my
advantage
and boy, does that seem to piss off
some of the other people in the room.

sometimes i wonder what my life were like if i didn't set myself up to be the rocks against which the brunt of everyone's emotional overload crashes on. sometimes i wonder what it would be like to be allowed to be the waves.

i don't think i would be waves
at this point.

the tide reels back and then
all of a sudden water
is a wall of its own,
reaching heights
of the tallest
skyscrapers
in the land
huh, land
i don't
think

much of that would be left over once my

tsunami crashes.

i can weather plenty;
when i was created,
i was created to be
formidable. strong.

unbreakable.

sometimes i wonder if you realise that you're slowly wearing at me, smoothing out my rough edges but also creating cracks in the surface that are running incredibly deep into the cavernous testaments of my very soul. sometimes i wonder if the only way you know how to bond with people is to wear them down so goddamn much that they

break

because you like handling the little pieces of what they used to be instead of standing back and admiring the larger picture that stands before you now.

sometimes i wonder…
…but wondering is useless.

wondering,

my love,
is a lost art form
that i have mastered
and have little use for.

maybe the catholic church was right
about idolizing false gods

I noticed that you ah
kept the beard.

You've kept the stubble,
You've shirked on shaving
daily
Your face isn't naked
like it was before we dated.

this probably wasn't even conscious,
and You've just gotten lazy again,
letting the days pass by
focused on other
aspects
of Your life...

because i imagine You're incredibly busy
now.

clearly, Your internship worked out
amazing,
and You were able to secure it for the
credits You need to graduate

and

You're having such an awesome time
at the house,
that i haven't seen You on campus
since that one day
two weeks ago
when i watched your side profile
bound away from the campus dunkin
and it took all of my restraint
not to shout out Your name
because i knew that if i did
and You looked at me
i would have

shattered.

i wish that i could actually
bring myself to hate You,
to actually mourn the loss of
You
but i fucking can't.

i only wind up hating myself,
hurting myself,
ripping scabs off of healing wounds
to make myself bleed and
feel something
again.

and You're...

unfazed.
unbothered.
living Your life as if not having me in it anymore
is one of the
best
damn
decisions
You've ever made.

i think i'm just mad that i cared.

i'm so
peeved
that the reason why i even started actually
talking
to Him
was because i would watch the two of you
hanging out
from the sidelines and
through the screen of my phone
and

He fucking took care of You.

He fucking took care of You
because that wasn't my place anymore.

You look better with the beard
anyways.

i'm glad You're keeping
something
and i hope...
i hope that sometimes
You feel the little ghosts of the way
my fingers used to run through
that beard of Yours,
play with it,
scratch the underside of Your chin
and make You laugh
because You thought that it was funny
whenever i did that.

the fall is over and i don't know what to do now

i told you how i felt
and
you don’t feel the same

but
it’s okay.

because i’ll take
whatever
place in your life
i can get.

www.ingramcontent.com/pod-product-compliance
Lightning Source LLC
Chambersburg PA
CBHW051735130826
49812CB00033B/869

* 9 7 8 9 3 5 7 4 4 6 8 1 5 *